Praise for Janet G Tharpe and *Such a God - Old Stories, New Voices*

Eli Wiesel contrasts Hebrew commentary on the Law, called *Halakah*, with Hebrew commentary on Biblical stories, called *Haggadah*. *Whereas 'Halakah' enjoins conformity by tracing guidelines to a way of life, Haggadah' is less severe and less coercive, and even at times, and as circumstances require, mischievous or poetic, awakens thought, meditation or prayer.* Tharpe offers contemporary *Haggadah*, a rehearing and resetting of biblical stories that are praise and provocation, full of humor, questions, anguish and faith. She has an audacious soul and a scintillating imagination. These prose poems will open you up. I commend them most highly to you. H. Stephen Shoemaker, retired pastor, visiting professor of religion at Johnson C. Smith University and author of several books, including, *Godstories: New Narratives from Sacred Texts*

Janet Tharpe knits into poems her deep awareness of the complex human condition, our broken creation and the always reaching out God. She puts the reader smack in the middle of this volatile mix. Her works startle and ring true, giving voice to the questions, longings and hopes we carry on our journeys. Janet Rittenhouse, Marriage and Family Therapist, Retreat Facilitator

The perspective that Dr. Tharpe has applied to these ancient stories has brought them into the present moment for me. I find them powerful as well as provocative. The title gives a much broader lens to the vision of Source including all sentient beings which touches my soul deeply.
Wendy Jo Johnson, LPCC Therapist/Artist/ Writer/ Seeker

One cannot read these poems without experiencing the freshness of perspective and relevance of faith-grappling with which Dr. Tharpe has imbued them. She has taken stories that we may know intimately and lifted them up to be examined in the prism of lived faith, doubt and ultimate wonder. She offers them to each of us for our journey. We find scripture illuminated. Thanks be.
Jim Rittenhouse, Assoc. Director of Music, St. Paul Methodist Church; Owner, McKinney Speakers Bureau

Dr. Tharpe's book is incredible. I have never been interested in poems; however, after reading a few of these, I was enthralled. She brings such a different perspective to mind by giving words, thoughts and actions to people, animals and even to objects that are ordinarily in the background. By doing so, she makes them key players. She certainly opened my eyes and shed a different and refreshing light on things that I thought I knew about! Adele Kleinhenz, Volunteer Liaison for Hosparus Grief Counseling Center

Janet Tharpe taps into her own creative birth rite. Using existing Biblical texts, her voice emerges and resonates with a sense of being present in that moment. This is no small thing. It is incarnational activity. She is a poet who is willing to be a birth giver.

Lou Ann Iler, Professional Artist /Teacher

Janet has a gift for bringing new images of ancient characters to life. Each brimming with new possibility, honesty, and a new interpretation. The reader will come away from these stories and poems with questions and wonderings that stir our perhaps stale imaginings of God's work in and through God's people – both from the ancient texts, and in our modern context. Nina, Maples Associate Pastor, Highland Baptist Church Louisville, Kentucky

SUCH A GOD

Old Stories, New Voices

JANET G THARPE

authorHOUSE®

AuthorHouse™
1663 Liberty Drive
Bloomington, IN 47403
www.authorhouse.com
Phone: 1 (800) 839-8640

Published by AuthorHouse   09/25/2015

ISBN: 978-1-5049-2964-6 (sc)
ISBN: 978-1-5049-2963-9 (e)

Library of Congress Control Number: 2015913360

Print information available on the last page.

Any people depicted in stock imagery provided by Thinkstock are models, and such images are being used for illustrative purposes only. Certain stock imagery © Thinkstock.

This book is printed on acid-free paper.

To the Crescent Hill Writers,
present and past:
You have helped me become a better writer
over the course of 30 years.
This book was born from your vision
and enthusiastic encouragement.
Thank you!

and

To Maggie "Mayhem" Mae
who dozed away for hours
under my desk and on top of my feet
while I pulled this book together.
Good dog!

CONTENTS

Acknowledgements

This book came into being through the skills, gifts and encouragement of many persons. I want to acknowledge and thank them here.

First, thanks goes all the good folks at AuthorHouse for helping me publish such an beautiful book.

Kudos go to Paul Burns, a talented graphic designer, who offered me eight beautiful choices for a book cover. It was a tough job choosing one but I finally selected the one you see.

Many thanks also go to Blake Ragsdell who was the Book Project Coordinator and Technical Assistant Extraordinaire. He patiently kept the tasks for getting published on track and moving forward. I was also fortunate to have back-up technical support from Lewis Miller who continues to help me with tasks like learning to blog and tweet. Many thanks, Lewis.

I am grateful for photographer Sam Springer of Springer Photography for going the extra mile to work with me and Maggie Mae to create a good picture for the book's back cover.

I want to thank Victoria Ragsdell who first planted the seed of the idea that the poems in these pages had the potential to become a book that would offer something unique and fresh to readers.

I also want to thank everyone who edited my manuscript at one time or the other: Rob Toney, Chuck Leach and Mrs. West, all current members of Crescent Hill Writers. Further editing was done on the manuscript including some last minute revisions by my friend, Ginger Miller.

Many thanks go to persons who took time out of their busy lives to read my manuscript and write endorsements: H. Stephen Shoemaker, Wendy Jo Johnson, Janet Rittenhouse, Lou Ann Iler, Adele Kleinhenz and Nina Maples.

And last, but not by any means least, my thanks goes to E. Frank. Tupper for writing the Foreword for my book. Dr. Tupper is a native of the Mississippi Delta and is a well-known preacher, teacher and author. His brilliant book *A Scandalous Providence: The Jesus Story of the Compassion of God*, first published in 1995 as a work in progress, was finished and revised into a New Edition in 2013. It reflects more than twenty years of academic research, theological reflection, and biographical pondering into a narrative rendering of the providence of God. Dr. Tupper is one of the founding faculty of the School of Divinity at Wake Forest University. He will retire next year to Louisville, KY.

FOREWORD

for *Such A God, Old Stories - New Voices*
by E. Frank Tupper, Ph.D.

Transposing Biblical stories into poetry is not unusual, but the powerful insights and creative imagination of Janet Tharpe's *Such A God - Old Stories, New Voices* is remarkably rare.

Testament One begins with sharp protests in the stories of human fallenness, first in the poem *It Seems Unfair To Me* where God is held responsible for setting up Adam and Eve to fail and then for creating such fierce arbitrary favoritism that the outcome is one of brother killing brother. In the poem *Such a God*, where God destroys all of life on earth except Noah's crew, the Ark itself expresses feeling ashamed. In *Babel* the promise of the rainbow is eclipsed. Judgments made in the poems *Pillar of Salt* and *Before Daybreak,* about Abraham and Lot and about the near sacrifice of Isaac respectively, presuppose the suppression of women and contain sharp feminist critiques. And while the story of Moses begins with creative beauty, the exodus includes indescribable grief. Finally, the arrogance of David is raised as a paradigm to the monarchical demise of kingdoms to come.

Testament Two describes the radical re-imaging of God in the compassionate story of Jesus' ministry, death, and resurrection. These poems resist a summary analysis. From the wedding feast at Cana to three brief accounts about daily bread, from the woman caught in adultery to the woman at the well, from the faith of the Roman centurion to the demonized Legion chained among the tombs, these encounters with Jesus disclose the healing love of God. The passion narratives are compelling renderings with layered depths of feeling, insight, and beauty. The *We Held the Space for Him* series of poems takes the reader through Holy Week from the joyful entry into Jerusalem, the agony in Gethsemane, the cross of God-forsakenness and finally the cold, granite tomb of death. The betrayal at the Passover table and the torn curtain—clothing the most holy area of the temple—stand alone: weighty, provocative, mirroring. Finally comes the painful, gentle, surprising testimony of the tomb, *I Could Hold Him No Longer.*

The storied poetry of Janet Tharpe revisions the reality of the Holy, the God who is love, but these historic testimonies require reading, rereading, and reading again—in silence and wonder.

INTRODUCTION

"Pickled," that is what my friend said about the stories in this collection. Many of us have heard these stories so often and for so long that they have become pickled for us. What a perfect metaphor! The stories are no longer fresh. We may think there is nothing left in them to discover or experience. We see them through the same lens each time we encounter them. However, whether these are pickled stories or are brand new to you, be forewarned: these are not Vacation Bible School Stories nor the Bible stories a parent reads at bedtime. However, if you are ready for a fresh adult perspective (different from the freshness of *Veggie Tales* which I also love) you have the right book in your hands. Here are a couple of examples. Have you ever imaged the story of Moses from the perspective of the bulrushes? (*Bulrushes: A Conversation*) Ever wondered about what the water Jesus turned into wine might have to say about *its* experience that day? (*In The Beginning, Cana*)

The poems in this book are written as prose poetry, which means each one has some attributes of both types of writing. This style has provided me with a way to engage creatively with the ancient narratives represented in these pages. I have imagined the stories being told by new voices that give expression to my discoveries, questions and astonishments. Take the story of Abraham who believed God told him to kill his son and offer him as a sacrifice. Is there anything in that story that disturbs you? It is one that has haunted me for as long as I can remember. So, in *Before Daybreak*, I give Abraham's wife, Sara, a voice so she can bear witness to the same event from her perspective and where she becomes a key player in the story's outcome. And what about the saga of Noah and the Great Flood? That is another troubling story for me. In the poem, *Such a God*, read what a tree, harvested and used in the construction of the ark has to say about its own unique involvement.

Some poems, like the *Daily Bread* series and the *We Held the Space* series in Testament Two are still shots, single frames within a larger moving story. There are a few poems where a character, with whom we are familiar, speaks, like God in *Babel* or Satan in *Daily Bread I*.

In preparation for writing these poems I did some research on cultural and contextual details in which the stories are wrapped.(*David's Slingshot*, *The Centurion* and *Qara*). All of that being said, I have done my best to remain true to the spirit of each story and as well as to the limitations of the perspective of the new voice telling it.

My hope for this small collection is to shift the paradigm of the way in which we have thought about these and other stories throughout our lives. It is my belief that by doing so we will find truths that are deeper and wider than we could ever imagine. I hope that as a result of exposure to these poems, readers will hear a new voice within themselves that opens up thoughts and feelings they may never have allowed themselves to imagine, let alone engage and ponder.

For anyone who is interested, the original texts from which these poems are created, are referenced in the Author's Notes at the end of this book.

TESTAMENT ONE

It Seems Unfair to Me

It seems unfair to me,
even cruel,
the way the landlord of Eden
set them up to fail,
placing one tree
with the loveliest,
most tantalizing fruit
right in their faces,
then saying *do not touch or else...*

The man, Adam
never forgave
Eve, the woman,
for giving him
the forbidden fruit.
He blames her
for the blisters he gets
and his back that aches
at the end of a long day
of warfare farming me,
the thorn-infested,
God-forsaken soil
outside of Paradise.

Out of her hot shame
and his cold rage
they conceive their first child,
a son they call Cain.
She delivers him
through the pain promised to her,
as her *or-else-consequence*
for touching what was
off limits in Eden.
Cain, though barely weaned,
works alongside his father,
desperate to win his approval.
Adam, himself an outcast,
had none to give.

The next male born,
they call Able, who
for reasons unknown
attracts not his father's
favor but that of God.

Maybe it is because
he is a keeper of
sheep and goats.
When he makes
an offering to God,
he selects one
and slits its throat.
Cain has nothing
so costly to offer,
just some potatoes,
a bag of dried beans,
a few turnips.

I think it no surprise
that Cain is jealous,
murderously so.
No matter how hard
he works, nothing
brings him validation.
So today Cain slit
Abel's throat;
I absorbed his blood.
Now he is afraid,
hearing God's voice
as he strolls over his
world at sunset.
Cain hides; God asks:
Where are you?
Where is your brother?
What have you done?

It seems unfair to me,
even cruel, the way
the landlord of Eden
set all of them up to fail.

Such a God

I stand tall in adoration,
my limbs extend into the sky.
My leafy hands tremble
as night flees before the dawn.
I hear shouting beneath me.
There is a frantic burst of activity.
What on earth is going on?
A blade strikes my timber
again and again and again,
until I fall helpless.
I grieve as my branches
are carelessly cut away from me.
An old man, hailed as Noah,
gives an order to drag me
to a staging area where
hundreds of my kind are
stripped naked, stacked,
and pounded into place,
one upon another, upon another.
We form an enormous box,
a crude, windowless shelter.
Little knots of people stand by
pointing and laughing while
a few rush to finish the building.
Now animals begin to arrive:
walking, wriggling, leaping, flying,
furred, feathered, scaly skinned,
seven of each and every kind.
The sky goes gray, releases rain,
pounding rain, merciless rain.
Rivers and streams are spilling over;
the wooden shelter starts to float.
It's door has been sealed and
a single family huddles inside
with wild, bewildered creatures.
Those who laughed do so no more;
instead they scream in terror,
scramble for higher ground.
This does not save them;
rising water overtakes them all.
Carcasses, human and animal,
float and bump against me.

I am adrift and ride the swells.
I overhear the Noah-man
referring to me and to my
gathered kindred as an ark,
commissioned by God to save
him alone and his family.
I look away and shiver, ashamed
to be a co-conspirator for
such a task by such a God.

THE WARRIOR'S BOW

סָאַן ת ֹ שֶׁק

ke-sheth saw-an

I watch him weep
with his head in his hands.
Today he declared war
on his disappointing creation.

He seizes me, סָאַן ת ֹ שֶׁק,
ke-sheth saw-an
his warrior bow.
We fire arrow after arrow,
like lightning bolts,
into a sky growing dark.
The arrows rip holes in the clouds,
unleashing an angry rain
that hammers, hammers down.
When he is exhausted,
he flings me with almighty fury
into a corner where I shatter.

The unmaking of
"in the beginning" begins.
Those who were created last,
who bear his own image,
are the first to drown,
helpless and panicked
in the rising water.
Yet, I can tell he is restless.
This course of action
has failed to bring him peace.
There is something in him
that cannot let all of it perish.

He keeps a watchful eye
on one tiny, terrified clan,
crowded into close quarters
with a collection of animals.
They bob about in the water
in a homemade wooden crate,
above the place that once
was the firmament, but is now
a watery wasteland.

Birds escape the earth
with flight and ride the wind,
until utterly spent they fall
into the flood waters.
Animals crazed with fear
can no longer find higher ground.
Plants, trees, flowers, all
are entombed beneath
the spreading water until
the distinctions between
the heavens and the earth
exist no more.

The sun, created to rule the day,
the moon and stars that
rule the night and govern time,
are extinguished.
Time stands still.
Once more the earth
...is without form and void;
darkness is upon
the face of the deep.
The Spirit of God broods
over the surface of the waters.

There is an eternity of silence.
Forty days and forty nights pass.
This is how long God grieves.
Then he reaches for me,
picks me up, holds me close.
He mends me, lifts me,
hangs me in the highest cloud.

He draw a deep breath and
clearing his throat; he speaks,
Let there be light!"

And there is light!
And oh, I am beautiful!

With the light shining
down through me

I see that I have been restrung
with five vibrant colors:
purple like distant mountains,
blue the color of robins' eggs,
green like verdant pastures,
yellow the color of the sun,
red the color of wild poppies.
I am a visual echo of every
color of creation!

God, repentant of his warring,
assigns to me a new purpose.
My job is to remind him to never
destroy his creation again.
The sight of me brings him peace.

Finally, God blesses me and
bestows my new name.
No longer am I a warrior's bow
I have become rain bow קֶ֫שֶׁת זֶ֫רֶם
ke'-sheth ze-rem
rainbow.

BABEL

They are at it again, my children.
I no sooner get the earth washed down
with a big flood, ready for a clean start,
and they are back at it,
joining their little lives together
to try to shape and insure their futures.
They bake clay bricks, mortar them into place
one upon another, one upon another.
Their tiny tower rises into the sky.
How do I get them stop the foolishness?
I don't have the stomach for another
mass murder by flood; besides
there is that rainbow promise I made;
and the kangaroos and big horned sheep
are just now really making a comeback.
Perhaps the children could be separated
from their collective arrogance.
I will jumble their words
into many different languages and
make them more afraid of each other
than they are of me.

PILLAR OF SALT, INDEED!

Pillar of Salt, indeed!
Never am I mentioned
by name, although
I have one!
I am only identified as
Lot's wife.

Lot and his Uncle Abraham
are two-of-a-kind,
both odd souls,
never able to stay long
in one place.
They took solace
in each other's company
and roamed for decades
the desert wastelands,
each with all his family,
animals and servants in tow.

One day Lot and Abraham
suddenly parted company.
I never really knew the reason;
but I have always believed it was
Abraham who instigated
our nomadic way of life.

Once separated and on our own,
we moved into a neighborhood
in the fixed city of Sodom.
Our wandering lifestyle ended.
For the first time in years
I was able to unpack completely,
get to know my neighbors,
make friends for keeps and
buy from the same merchants
in the same marketplace daily.
In no time at all
I established daily routines
for the running of my household.

Weeks and then months passed.
Our lives were settled and content,
until Lot brought home
two men, traveling strangers,
he met at the city's gate.
As is our custom, he offered them
hospitality: a meal and safe lodging
in our home for the night.

I made the evening meal a feast;
the table conversation was lively.
In order to give our guests
room to sleep indoors,
I tell my daughters
they can sleep on the roof overnight.
Both girls squeal and hop around,
giddy with excitement about
this rare sleep-over.
They carry an oil lamp and some
bedding up onto the roof while
I finish cleaning supper dishes
and relax into the sweet peacefulness
of the day drawing to a close.

BAM! BAM! BAM!
Someone sounds angry
banging on our front door.
I can hear muffled voices
from a mob out in our yard.
Alarmed, I freeze in place.

Lot cracks the front door open,
squeezes out and is met
with a roar of demands
to hand over our guests.
The crowd insists they are
entitled to take custody of them,
to do with them as they please.
I hear Lot shout, *I will not!*
Then I hear him try
to strike a bargain
so he will not be guilty of
violating the code of hospitality.
He offers the mob
our daughters instead.

I pull my girls tight against me,
hope they have not heard him
and tell myself he is in for
a long talk later about that idea!

It takes our two guests
and myself to pull Lot
back inside where we
barricade every door
and every window.
Hours pass and finally
the angry mob loses interest,
grows weary of their siege
and gradually disperses.

The six of us huddle together through
an uneasy night; no one sleeps.
We ask each other in whispers,
Will they come back tonight?
What will happen in the morning?

I grow irritated with our guests.
They are frightening the children,
saying, *We will have run for our lives*
at first light; God has it in for Sodom.
He is going to destroy the city because
he is displeased with the city's failure
to provide common hospitality.

All I can think about is
I don't want to leave my home.
I say to Lot quietly,
They can't be serious.
Yet, he believes they are.
We have no time to pack;
besides how could we
run for our lives if we
carried our belongings?

It starts to sink in,
there will be no chance
for good-byes with my friends,
no time to return the soup pot
I borrowed from my neighbor;
no time to give another neighbor
the recipe she asked for.
I grow even more sick at heart
with the realization that I will
have no opportunity
to warn any of them about
God's impending
plan for destruction.

When a sliver of light
begins to stretch across
the horizon,
our guests warnings
become more urgent.
Each of them takes
one of our girls to carry
on their backs and
hurries out the door.
I am right behind them.
There is no way I am going
to let the girls out of my sight!
We move furtively,
silent as shadows,
through the empty streets.
Once outside the city gate,
I stop to catch my breath.
The two guests insist that we
move on, move away
from the city wall,
out to some low hills
in the distance.

They leave us
with one last warning,.
As you go, do not look back
or you will be consumed.
Consumed? I am already consumed!
Overwhelmed! Flooded with feelings!

I need some time to say
some sort of good-bye,
a few minutes to ponder my losses,
some kind of closure to
the abrupt ending into which
we have been so hastily hurled.

I walk until I think I have come
a safe distance from Sodom.
Deliberately I turn around for
one last look at what was home.
Yes, I have a name, but I am
known only as *Lot's wife,*
the woman who looked back,
who did not flinch or turn away,
who watched a holocaust
of sulfur and fire rain down
on sweet friends and their children
at the whim of a short-tempered God.

I am the eye witness to what took place.
I hold the sacred memory of Sodom
and those who perished there
preserved in my heart, as if with salt.
Pillar of Salt?
Indeed

Before Daybreak

Before daybreak
they take their leave,
my odd, old headstrong husband
and our only child, struggling
to keep up with his father's pace.

Standing in the doorway of our tent
I watch them go, still trembling at
Abraham's parting words to me.
Leaning down, he rests his
scratchy, bearded check
against my smooth one and
whispers in my ear,
God has directed me to sacrifice
the boy on the Mountain; so we go.

What madness had come over him!
How come God did not tell me, too?
I am dazed. Enraged! Horrified!
Then a determined calm settles on me;
I resolve to rescue my son.

I gather half a dozen rams
to take with me on my mission.
Using a different route, I remain
undetected through sleepless nights
never stopping long, unable to rest.

Relieved to reach the summit first,
I quickly tie rams scattered
in the underbrush where I also hide.
It is early afternoon when Abraham
appears carrying the fire and the knife.

Minutes later Isaac trudges into view
breathing hard, carrying on his back
all the wood for the alter fire that will
consume the corpse of whatever is
slaughtered there as an offering to God.

I hear Isaac ask his father
Where is the animal
for our sacrifice?
The monotone reply,
God will provide.

My heart is in my throat when next
he says, *Hold out your hands, son,*
I need to bind them.
Then he lifts the boy onto the alter,
coaxes him to lie still.

The two of them seem to move
before me in slow motion;
a dull-eyed man and a child
whose eyes are wide with terror
watching his father raise the knife.

I grab the ram tied closest to me
and bury my face and my scream
in its thick wool.
It bleats loudly in protest,
and Abraham pauses.

With his knife stopped in mid-air,
he looks around as if
he expects to see God,
but there is only rustling
underbrush and a struggling ram.

He comes for the animal,
and though he is quite near to me,
I manage to remain unseen.
He replaces Isaac with the ram
upon the waiting alter.

Abraham looks heavenward,
raises the blade once more,
oblivious to his trembling son
backing away from him
rubbing the rope burns on his wrists.

THE BULRUSHES IN CONVERSATION

The princess is early today and alone.

> Hmmm. She usually comes later
> in the morning to bathe.

Oh, my mistake;
it's not her.

> That one looks more like one of those Hebrew
> slave girls to me, couldn't be more than 13 years old.

> > *Why is she bending over*
> > *carrying that covered basket*
> > *that way?*

> I don't know; most women carry
> a load like that on their head.

Why do you think she stops so often and
crawls under the cover of those tall grasses?

> > *Probably just resting.*

No I think she hiding. She looks scared
and she keeps looking back as if
she is afraid of being followed.

> What do you think is in the basket?

I don't know but she is
putting it into the river.

> Oh My Goodness!
> > *LOOK IT FLOATS!*

> It bobs around like a little boat!

Obviously it has been cleverly
designed and sealed

> > *Hey where'd the girl go,*
> > *did she leave?*

> She's over there in the spare shade
> of those scrubby shrubs hiding

She seems to have settled in
to keep an eye on the wee basket.

--Later the same morning—

Hey heads up everyone
here come the princess with her entourage!

I can always hear them coming before I see them,
all talk and laughter.

Do you think the princess can see the basket
from the river bank?

I don't think so.

Maybe she will when she gets
gets into the water.

Now she does!

See, she is pointing at it and
one of her attendants is wading out to get it.

Surely we will know soon just what
is in the little flotsam now resting at
the princess' feet awaiting her inspection.

Oh my something in it is moving.

Do you hear a baby fussing?

Don't be absurd;
couldn't be a baby
Could it?

What are they all looking at?
They're all bent over
peering into the basket,
smiling so big they are like one big happy face

It IS a baby!
They are passing it around.

I think the princess has
forgotten her bath entirely.

Hush!
I want to hear what they are saying.

Where did he
-yes it's a he-
come from?

Who left him here?

I think he is a Hebrew baby

The princess declares,
I am going to keep him and
raise him as a prince!

Over there,
that girl who was hiding is getting up
and walking toward he princess.

What on earth do you think she will say?

I can barely hear her
she speaks so softly.

Your Highness,
I know a Hebrew woman
who could nurse the baby
for you
until he is weaned.

Splendid idea!
Go get her girl and
bring her to me!

--MANY YEARS LATER—

Look there everyone!
through the morning mist,
I think the princess is approaching!

She walks alone
and staggers.

She has not been here in many years,
not since she was a young woman.

Do you remember the day
she found that baby in a basket?

How could any of us forget that day?

And she used to bring the boy here
to bathe him, then later to teach
him how to swim

He never got
very good at it.

No he never did.

Listen she is sobbing.

What could make a princess
weep so inconsolably?

Did you not hear the news
last night on the mid-night wind?

Do you mean what the Pharaoh's dogs
were howling about?

Yes, but I thought it was
just a horrible nightmare.

Horrible? Yes, but not a nightmare.
This morning the princess mourns
the death of her oldest child and
the death of her first grandchild.

CROSSING OVER

Ha! We have them now!
Their backs are to the sea!
They can see us approaching.
Fathers clutch crying children,
mothers' faces go bloodless.
Their terror is tangible.
They stand defenselss before us!
Mighty and menacing are we!
Our hooves strike the ground,
raising dust and thunder!
Our nostrils flare!
We suck down burning air!
Our lungs are on fire!
Those slaves will rue the day
they fled the Pharoah's favor!
There is no escaping us;
we, are the on-coming consequence
of their running away.

A rogue wind begins to blow;
it grows stonger as we
close the gap between us and
the helplessly huddled.
We are alarmed.
We slow to a trot.
The sea is peeling back,
creating two walls of water
and a dry place to walk
right between them
over to the other shore!

The runaways rush to cross over,
pushing and shoving each other,
dragging their belongings,
along with their sheep and goats,
their donkeys and chickens.

We recover from our shock and
plunge into the same passageway
between the walls of water.
Half way across we bog down.
What had been a firm passage way
softens into a muddy quagmire.

We strain with all our might;
yet we can no longer pull
the weight of our chariots.
It is impossible to move.
The walls become liquid
and disgorge the power
they were holding back.
As they collapse,
the water covers us.
And so we perish,
in our harnesses,
anchored to
the floor of the sea.

David's Slingshot

I am not celebrated like
the shepherd boy's harp.
I am not beautiful and
there is nothing about me
to reflect my superiority.
However, in this crisis,
it is me he has chosen
to accompany him here.
It is I who wait on the top of
a pile of my poor boy's clothing,
on a dirt floor swept smooth
in the tent of King Saul.

My boy is trying on the King's
bronze helmet which
slides down over his eyes.
Under the weight of
the King's chain mail
he staggers as if drunk.
When he raises the King's sword,
he nearly falls over.
The king's armor does not fit;
it reeks of vanity

With youthful confidence.
my boy declines
the terrified king's offer
to loan his own wardrobe and
weapons for war,
for a duel to the death,
a winner-take-all proposition,
made by a mountain of a man,
a filthy Philistine.

My boy slips back into his own clothes,
picks me up and tells the King
The Lord who delivered me
from the teeth of the bear and
from the claw of the lion when
I was protecting my father's sheep
will fight and win this day
for the army of Israel!

THAT'S MY DAVID!
I want him to tell the King
about us and our exploits,
but he chooses to withhold
the bravado, a little bit
intimidated I guess,
standing in the royal court

What he does not say is
we win most slingshot contests
back home, including contests
arranged by bored soldiers
on leave looking for something
to do to pass the time.
We have bested many of them,
even though many are trained
to use slingshots in battle.
The truth is we can hit
a pomegranate target,
on a boulder fifty yards away.

We take our leave of Saul's tent
to walk along the creek
that runs behind the ranks
of Israel's army.
We search for stones with
just the right shape and heft.
We find five and the boy
puts them in the pouch
he has tied around his waist.

Once we pick our way through
the lines of the King's army,
we emerge and stand face to face,
with a giant soldier named Goliath
who is shouting taunts and jeers
at the overwhelmed army of the King.
My boy, shouts up to him:
You have come to me with a sword
and a spear, but I come to you in
in the name of the Lord of hosts
whose army you are defying.
Know that this very day, he will
deliver you into my hands,
and I will give your bones and
the bones of your army
to the birds and the wild animals.

Goliath guffaws at David's speech,
such words from the mouth of a mere boy
whose voice has not yet changed.
David retrieves a stone.
He positions it within me and
starts to swing me around above
his head: once, twice, three times,
then too many, too rapid
to keep up the count.

When speed and aim are perfect,
he releases the stone to flight.
Goliath takes the hit squarely
between his eyes which close;
his knees buckle and he collapses
onto the ground, out cold.
My David then uses Goliath's
own sword to finish him off.
The defeat of their giant
causes the Philistine army
to break ranks and run in full retreat.

-----------------SOME YEARS LATER----------------

Today David is King and
once again is facing down
swaggering arrogance,
only this time it is his own.
He meets with the prophet Nathan,
who fells the King with a word,
Thou art the man.

TESTAMENT TWO

DAILY BREAD I

I've been watching you.
I can hear the rumble and
growl of your empty belly.
How long has it been?
40 days? Wow!
You are looking thin.
You need your strength.
Look at those stones;
they look like loaves of bread
warm from the oven.
They could be, too,
if you just say the word.
No one will ever know
except you and me.

In the Beginning, Cana

In cold and quiet darkness I waited,
a pooled power of life-giving liquid,
resting reticent in the recesses of earth.
Then, hailed for, I am hauled out,
drawn up in a bucking bucket,
casually and carelessly.
I ascend from my expansive earthen cavern
to be a contained, a cramped captive,
in one of six waiting water jars.

I am poured, splashing and swirling
into the cool clay interior of a tall vessel,
solid and wide-brimmed.
I settle swiftly into its shape,
sending topside remnants of racing ripples
until at last I stand utterly stilled,
with sunlight skipping and
shimmering across my glassy surface.

Nearby a Presence hovers and broods
sending an involuntary shiver of
unexpected anticipation through me.
Then ancient eyes reflect their own
depths on my humble face
and I recognize Ruach's face!
Thus beheld, knowing and known, I blush,
and become the blessing of wedding wine:
I, the element of his first miracle, again!

ALWAYS

I lay at peace, basking, content
on this warm, sunny day.
I lounge among my brothers,
in the shadow cast across us
by The Gentle One.
In the distance, I hear
a disturbance beginning:
It is a dreadful sound
headed my way,
familiar voices, angry harsh
and hell-bent on
declaring and delivering justice.
Today the group of men bring a
terrified, weeping woman.
They stop close to me,
surge forward all together,
convulse and draw back,
expelling her like vomit
from their midst.
Shoved into the center
of a shallow pit, her knees
betray her legs' bid to stand.

A large, sweaty hand
snatches me up,
waves me wildly overhead.
The mob grows louder
shouting and cursing.
I know what comes next.
I and those like me will be
collected and hurled at the
woman to bruise her
and make her bleed,
to shatter her teeth
and break her bones.
In the end we will be left
covering her lifeless body.

But wait! Today there is
an interruption in the process
to which I am accustomed.

The mob quiets,
pauses, waits while
the religious leaders
quiz The Gentle One.

In taunting tones they say,
We caught her red faced
in the unholy act of adultery.
The law says to stone her
to death; what do you
have to say on the matter?

He does not look at the faces
of those who challenge him.
His eyes rest softly upon
her small figure, on her knees,
curled over, face touching the ground.

He gives his answer with authority
and yet almost under his breath,
I say that only the one among you
who has never done wrong
must throw the first stone.

He squats down where he stands,
drags his fingers through the dirt.
The sweaty hand that holds me
allows me to drop the ground.
The mob leaves silently, slowly,
one by one by one by one.

Once all of them are gone,
he stands, steps down into the pit,
stretches out his hand and
takes the woman's arm, lifting her.
He looks into her face and asks
with a fierce tenderness,
Where are those who brought
you here to execute you?
She glances around,
Her lower lip quivers; she replies
Gone, sir. They have all gone.
He says to her, *I release you also;.*
Go your way. Live in the light.

I will never forget
this day at the stoning pit.
Even if no one else remembers,
I, steadfast as a stone,
will always remember.
Always.

DAILY BREAD II

This crowd has been here
listening to him for three days!
Now they are grumbling
about being hungry.
He should have sent them home
yesterday or the day before.
Wait! Why are they sitting down?
He did? And then feed them?
All five thousand of them?
Surly he has been misunderstood!
We don't have food for ourselves.
Can we make bread from stones?
Who keeps tugging on my robe?
Oh, it's just a small child smiling,
holding up a little basket with
seven loaves and two tiny fish.

Living Water

Every day around noon
she comes to find me;
Her hands are warm
on my cool clay surface.
If there is water left in me,
she pours it on her herbs,
growing in pots on the patio.
Then, as is our custom,
we make our way to the well
beyond the boundaries of town,
out a hundred yards or more
to draw up a day's worth of water.

Today she is as intensely isolated
inside her own thoughts
as she is separated
from the others of her kind,
women who trek to the well
in coolness of early morning.
For them she is a gossip staple
to be shunned and shamed.

It is only when we are
a few yards away
that she sees him
sitting on the ground,
leaning against the well.
In mid-stride we stop.
She regards him with
a scornful stare while
assessing what kind of trouble
this man might make for her.

With his hands he shades
his eyes to look at us and
grimaces in the glare of noon.
His appearance is grizzled;
for an instant our gazes lock.
Like one who is weary,
he struggles to his feet,
licking dry, sunburned lips.

We take a step back,
her grip on me tightens.
In a moment of resolve
she squares her shoulders,
marches forward with authority,
and sets me down firmly
beside the ancient well.

He coughs, chokes, clears his throat.
then croaks out, *I am thirsty.*
Can I trouble you for a drink of water?
She retorts *Jew, you do not belong here!*
Why are you so far from your own country?

She shifts uneasily when he replies,
We are from the same place you and I,
both cast out by our own kin and clan,
transgressors of the Law according to
the pious and religious who interpret it.
We are both out of step with those
who believe they are the sole possessors
of what is right and of what is sacred.

Her suspicion softens some.
She knows the role of outcast,
a label that has clung to her
through five husbands and
the man with whom she now lives,
a man she has not married.

He continues to speak to her
Do you know who I am?
If you did you would ask me for water.
His voice is hoarse, coarse,
I have living water that quenches
thirst forever with one deep drink
In fact he says, *it brings eternal life.*

Now I think he has gone too far!
He is trying to play her for a fool.
She will not buy into promises
far too good to be true.

So, I remain solidly skeptical.
After all, the only thing I know
about him is he does not have
the means to get a drink of water
from a well right beneath his feet.
Yet she seems compelled to listen
to him as he tells her own story to her,
reviewed with boundless compassion.
In a hushed voice she dares to say,
I have heard of a prophet coming,....
someone who will speak as you do....
He answers the question
she cannot bring herself to ask,
I am he, the one speaking to you now.

He suggests she return to town
and bring back all of her neighbors,
who have treated her
like she was dung
or worse, invisible.
Bring them to meet the prophet,
the foreigner who has
told you everything about your life.

She heads back to town, running.
In her excitement she leaves me
with the strange Jew,
who with my assistance,
finally gets a drink of water.

Soon, in the distance I see
a wave of people flooding
out from town,
pouring in our direction,
eager, I assume, to acquire
the mysterious living water
that would banish thirst forever,
and bestow eternal life.

Living water, as it turns out,
is mostly about a way of living:
doing justice, practicing mercy
and walking humbly with God,
so that no soul need never perish
again from a drought of any kind.

The stranger stayed in town
with us two more days
and carried me to and from
the well each morning.
On the third day he moved on.

THE CENTURION

I wake and find
Alexander shivering beside me.
The sweat beading on his boyish brow
is evidence of a fever.
He is my companion, has been
for three years, since he was 16.
He is my confidant, my beloved.

I pull him closer to me,
wrap him in my arms,
stroke his damp hair.
At sunrise he begins
convulsing in a seizure
so violent he is left paralyzed,
open-eyed and terrified.

I am afraid also; my hands tremble.
Under my breath I curse
this tiny, troublesome,
God-forsaken place where
Rome sent us to keep the peace.

My mind races, *what to do?*
I remember rumors about
a local carpenter turned healer.
The gossip is that he is
staying nearby; *would he help me?*

I pile every available blanket
on Alexander, moisten his lips
with a bit of water,
kiss his cheek,
go to find my commanding officer,
request permission to leave the post,
seek out this healer and
implore him to come back with me
before it is too late.

My commander offers
to send a slave for the menial task
of summoning someone.
I decline; I must go myself.

Choking back my fears
I ride hard on horseback
to the last known whereabouts
of the Carpenter turned Healer.
Arriving in coastal Capernaum,
I smell the catch of the day
weighing heavy on the air
as the fish are removed
from the fishermen's nets.

Where a crowd is gathered,
I dismount in a cloud of dust,
push others aside with
an authority born of desperation.
I see him and he sees me.
His eyes are deep pools
reflecting power and mercy.
He knows why I have come
before I ever speak a word.

He offers to go back with me.
I say to him, *No, that is not necessary.*
My soldiers obey my orders when I give them.
here in your presence
I know that is enough for you
to speak words of healing.

We embrace and I leave
puzzled about his remarks
to the crowd about my faith,
like it was something rare
or remarkable, when it was
simply, all that I had.

Back on post, I find Alexander
preparing my noon meal.
With relief and deep gratitude
I hug him to me and weep.

UNTIL TODAY

Neither of us are welcome in the villages;
no one has any use for either of us.
He is a massive mad man no chain can hold;
we, the cloven hooved, declared unclean.
And so we live as neighbors
upon these high cliffs, above the sea,
far from the limits of tiny towns.

People gave up trying to manage him
and long ago abandoned him here,
among the tombstones in this graveyard.
Each day he roams, naked and restless,
maniacally muttering to himself.
Who knows what he is saying.
He drags a short length of chain
attached to an ankle cuff that
still remains locked on him.
It gives him a distinctive sounding gait.
Often we startle when he shrieks,
but we do not fear him.
Sometimes he cuts himself with sharp rocks,
it seems to soothe him somehow,
and then bleeding,
he will lie down whimpering,
grow quiet and sleep

He calls himself Legion, meaning many.
We are many as well;
our number is almost two thousand.
Neither he nor us are fit to look upon,
our appearances are un-kept:
his beard and his hair
are long, matted, tangled.
Our skins are rough and dirty.
We smell much the same,
of animal musk and excrement.

No one visits him.
We are his only companions.
We share with him the roots
we forge from beneath rocky soil.

In turn he shares the table scraps
that a kind crone sometimes
sets out for him from a safe distance
before she hurries away.
Today had been peaceful enough
until a little knot of fishermen
left a couple of small boats
at the edge of the water
and worked their way up the cliff.

The moment the Legion
catches sight of them
he squats to hide
behind a grave stone.
He rocks and mumbles frantically.
One of the men from the boats,
the one with Soft Eyes, approaches him.
Legion lunges toward him,
screeching with rage and
ripping out hair from his own scalp.
What do you have to do with me
Jesus Son of the Most High God?
Leave me alone! Go away! GO AWAY!

With a whispered command Soft Eyes
speaks, *Unclean spirits come out of him.*
Then gently as if to a child who is lost,
What is your name?
Do not torment us Legions' demons plead.
Preferring banishment to annihilation,
Soft Eyes gives them permission
and instruction,
You may enter that herd of pigs over there.

Howling the unclean spirits
leave Legion and settle on us.
Their madness drives us all
over the cliff and into the sea.
where most of us drown.

We are not sacred animals
in any way whatsoever,
never have been.
Our young are not taken to the temple,
to be used as a sacrifice or an offering.
We have no part in festivals or feasts
and have existed without purpose
for thousands of years until today,
when we died to restore
one man's mind.

DAILY BREAD III

Martha's making bread this morning
and I lie awake,
listening to the soft thud
as she throws the dough
onto the rough wooden table.
I can picture the little cloud
of flour that rises around it
each time it hits the table's surface..
She slept not at all last night,
too wondrously disturbed by
by my being alive again,
called back from the dead.
This morning she is held and
comforted in her familiar routine.
It is something she can count on.

Holy Week: We Held the Space for Him

THE PALMS

That day, freshly cut and green
we held the space for him.
Scattered with abandon
as he approached,
we lined a narrow pathway
through the excited crowd.
Some people threw down their
clothing, caught up in the moment.
Curious, they pushed forward
to catch a glimpse of him.
That day we held the space for him,
a space he could pass through.

THE OLIVE TREES OF GETHSEMANE

On that night of angst and agony
when a wild wind blew,
we held the space for him.
Among our ancient, twisted trunks,
beneath our gnarled branches,
utterly heart-broken and alone,
he moved between seeking the
solace of solitary prayer and
the comfort of his sleepy,
uncomprehending companions.
We held the space for him
until a rogue mob took him away.

The Cross of Golgotha

At mid-day, when the sun was eclipsed,
I held the space for Him to die.
His arms were taut and out-of-joint
across my horizontal beam while
He hung, slowly suffocating
upon my vertical timber.
In a fevered pitch of pain,
He cried, *My God,*
why You forsaken me?
I held the space for Him to die
until He wheezed,*it is finished.*

Garden Tomb

That evening, before the Sabbath,
I held the space for him.
His rigid, naked body,
broken and battered
almost beyond recognition,
was laid within the silence
of my cool stone interior
and secured by a boulder
that sealed my doorway.
I held the space for him.

I Am the Table

Over the years, I have had
the honor of hosting pilgrims
who come from near and far
to this city to celebrate
this high holiday called Passover.
I know well the ritual
with the embedded meal;
it makes for a long evening.
Often I gather large families;
but those finding their seats
beside me tonight are not kin,
though they behave in the same way.
They call out loud greetings,
slap each other on the back,
laugh at inside jokes, use nicknames.
And as always, there is one
who keeps his own counsel
and remains on the margins.

An hour or so into the feast
I become aware of fingers
drumming on my surface.
The group's leader notices, too,
and announces, *One who is*
at this table will soon betray me.
Shocked whispers buzz above me,
almost everyone is asking,
Will it be me? Do you mean me?
The finger drummer stops,
places both of his hands
palms down upon my surface,
leans into the face of the host
with a posture that
all but dares him
to out him to the others.
He growls, *Will it be me?*
The response comes quietly,
Go. Carry out your plans.
He leaves quickly without
a word of departure.

The leader stands, picks up
a flat piece of bread and the
cup of wine reserved for Elijah.
Hold it! I know the liturgy of
this night; this is not how it goes.
He says something peculiar.
This bread and cup,
are for you as a way to remember me
as flesh and blood among you.
Whenever you share them together,
I will be near you.
They sang the traditional psalm
and filed out into the darkness
without a word.

I am the table around which
this band of thirteen gathered.
I wonder what will become of
of the one who left early and
of the leader who
claimed Elijah's cup.

QARA

Splendid I am and beautiful,
crafted from the finest
hand-woven wool,
dyed a deep royal purple,
embroidered with scarlet thread.

Worthy to clothe a Deity am I.
Fifty golden clasps
suspend me in place
between the Temple's
restricted Holy of Holies
and the wide stone gate
through which the masses
stream into the outer courts.

Today is unfathomable;
darkness falls at mid-day.
God's beloved is executed
publicly: bloodied, bruised,
broken and naked upon a cross.

When his son breathes his last,
God, wild with a parent's grief,
seizes me and rips me in two
top to bottom as a sign of anguish,
just like Jacob tore his clothing
when he learned of Joseph's death.

I Could Hold Him No Longer

No hope remains now.
His bloodied body
is carried into
my granite womb.
I want to weep
when his last two friends
leave his lifeless body
within me, upon a carved
slab of rock, as if on a lap.
They leave him
tucked in safely
with a boulder blocking
the doorway.

Two days pass;
he remains stiff and cold.
Still I hold His flesh
with fierce tenderness,
like a mother holding
her newborn child.
Then suddenly today,
the third day,
his heart warms,
begins to beat!
His chest rises gently;
he began to draw breath!

He labors and rests,
labors and rests,
shedding his grave linens,
like a butterfly does
its cramped cocoon,
until at last he stands.

I shiver and
dislodge the rock
that seals the doorway.
I can hold him no longer.
He steps out
into a garden, unbound
unhindered, forever alive.

Author's Notes

The following notations provide information about where the story being referenced can be found. There is also some additional information about selected poems.

TESTAMENT ONE

It Seems Unfair to Me
Genesis 3:17 – 4:10 [4:10]

Such a God
Genesis 6:11-17, 7:1-4 and 7:17-24

The Warrior's Bow
Genesis 9:13

In the Hebrew language, the word for a bow [ke-sheth saw-an] and the word for rainbow [ke'-sheth ze-rem] share in common the rendering of the word bow.

It may be noted that the God of this poem is the same God who from time to time throughout history has changed a person's name when they were called on for a new purpose or task. A few examples include: Abram to Abraham, Sarai to Sarah, Jacob to Israel and Simon to Peter. In this poem, God changes the name and purpose of the warrior's bow, an instrument of violence, to the rainbow, a sign of God's covenant of peace.

The Bullrushes In Conversation
Exodus 2:1-10 and 11:4-5

Before Daybreak
Genesis 22:1 – 13

Pillar of Salt
Genesis 19: 1 – 26, specifically verse 26
The author would like to nominate "Lot's wife" as the patron saint for all first responders.

Crossing Over
Exodus 14:8 – 30

David's
I Samuel 17:32 – 51 and 2 Samuel 12:1-7

TESTAMENT TWO

In the Beginning, Cana
John 2:1 – 12 Ruach (roo-auk) is the Hebrew word for the Spirit that
brooded over the waters in the Creation Story in Genesis 1:2.

In 1986, this poem won the first place award in the Bible category
sponsored by Ruth Meyer Morton as part of the Kentucky State Poetry
Society's annual contest. It was first published the same year in *Pegasus*
along with the other contest winners.

Daily Bread I
Luke 4:1 -4 specifically verse 3

Daily Bread
Matthew 15:29-38

Living Water
John 4:1- 43

The Centurion
Matthew 8:5-13
For more on this perspective on the cultural norm with regard to deployed
Roman officers and their servants. http://www.wouldjesusdiscriminate.
org/biblical_/evidence/gay/couple.html

Until Today
Mark 5:1 – 15

Daily Bread
John 11:39, 43-44

We Held the Space
To "hold the space" means to be mindful of the present time
or place with the awareness that it is infused with the sacred.

The Palms Mark 11:7 – 8
The Olive Trees Mark 14:32 – 42
The Cross John 19:16 – 18
The Tomb Luke 23:50-54

I Am the Table
Matthew 26:20 – 30

During Passover, the Seder table is prepared and decorated with symbols
that serve as reminders to Jewish celebrates what it was like to be a slave
under the Pharaoh in Egypt and about their hasty departure when they
were finally released. One of those symbols is a cup filled with wine that
is set on the table for the prophet Elijah. Elijah was a mighty a prophet
who was expected to return prior to the coming of the Messiah. For me
to suggest that was the cup Jesus picked up and offered to his disciples
in the Upper Room on the eve of the cross is to suggest he was saying to
them that Elijah had come and was even present with them in the room
and that *the great and terrible day of the Lord was at hand.* (Malachi 4:5)

Qara
Luke 23:45 *Qara* (kaw-rah) is the verb that describes the Jewish ritual of
tearing one's garments when mourning. The same word is used in both
of the references below:

and while the sun's light failed, the curtain of the
Temple was torn in two. Luke 23:45

Now Jacob tore his garments...and mourned for
[Joseph] for many days. Genesis 37:34

In 2004, this poem won the first place award in the Bible category
sponsored by Ruth Meyer Morton as part of the Kentucky State Poetry
Society's annual contest. It was first published
the same year in *Pegasus* along with the other contest winners.

I Could Hold Him No Longer
Mark 16:1 – 6

Author's Contact Information

To learn about my new projects or how to schedule me for a reading and/or discussion about Such A God, see my web-page at janetgtharpe. wordpress.com. You can leave your contact information for me there and I will get back to you. There is also information there about how to order more copies of Such A God.

Printed in the United States
By Bookmasters